Capitalism Must Be Composted

OTHER BOOKS BY RUTH OSKOLKOFF

Sacramentals
These 21 poems are detailed observations of Seattle's rain, mist, parks, gardens, and people and the daily elements that make life sacred. The images span an eclectic mix: a day at the market, a child at the grocery store, watching rain on rivers, or a celebration of seemingly ordinary objects on a mantle.

Detained
This political collection offers 21 sparkling little gems of poetry in the lyric tradition. Brief, full of authentic feeling, with lines that are more like a song. Includes poems about nature, death, love, and revolution.

Voyage to the Sun: A Children's Version of the Tao te Ching
The pages contain ideas present in the original Tao - but simplified for children. This book is about kindness, our shared humanity, recognizing natural patterns, to look for the subtle and the nuanced, and to think for ourselves. It encourages children to put aside hate and take steps to be a bold influence in the world. To have courage. Features whimsical art by Joan Hunter Iovino.

Books available on Amazon

Capitalism Must Be Composted

Quotes for Gardeners, Lovers, Activists, and Allies

Ruth Oskolkoff, Editor
Sneha Sinha, Artist

Copyright © 2018 Ruth Oskolkoff

All rights reserved. Except for brief passages quoted in a newspaper, magazine, radio, television review or other media, no part of this book may be reproduced in any form or by any means, electronic or mechanical, including photocopying and recording, or by any information storage and retrieval system, without permission in writing from the authors and artist.

ISBN-13: 978-1-7310-2625-5

DEDICATION

This book is for activists everywhere. Both
known and unknown. Those dying alone in a prison
cell, or tortured with no one to help and also those
who live in a comfortable house in a peaceful land.
Those who are part of a group and those also who
have no comrades to help them change society. Our
words are just as brilliant as the famous, the rich,
the lauded, or the powerful. We are the people.
We are the leaders. We are the stars.

CONTENTS

FOREWORD i
PREFACE v
ACKNOWLEDGEMENTS vii
EPIGRAPH ix
ABBREVIATIONS xi
Quotes for Gardeners, Lovers, Activists, and Allies 1
List of Contributors 163
About the Editor and Artist 165

FOREWORD

A funny thing happened in the very long lead up to the 2016 election. Facebook provided a medium for Americans to talk to each other in a way we'd never done before. Some of us had woken up a long time ago. Some of us woke up during the 2016 primaries. Some of us are hoping and trying to get others to wake up. We even invented a new word – woke. We are woke. We know what is going on, and we're not going to take it anymore.

It was exciting when many of us got behind Bernie Sanders. At first it was a long shot, and then the excitement grew. More people joined and his rallies were huge. We even got a sign – the bird that landed on his podium at Portland in March of 2016.

We were part of a movement that was going to change the world. We got organized and elected progressive delegates to represent us at the Democratic National Convention. We contributed our time and energy and money to Bernie Sanders and other candidates. We elected delegates and raised money to get them to Philadelphia.

There were disturbing signs from early on – people were turned away from caucuses and there were crazy coin tosses. Voter registrations disappeared, and people were obstructed from voting in various ways. The Nevada State Democratic Convention in Las Vegas was the culmination of the chaos surrounding the primaries.

We were falsely accused of throwing chairs, and Barbara Boxer gave us the finger. Many of our Bernie groups were slammed with porn and shut down by Facebook the night before the California primary. And while all this excitement was building, the mainstream media (MSM) ignored our candidate and pretended our movement didn't exist.

Despite all that, we still believed we could prevail. Our delegates went to Philadelphia, and so did many of us. Thanks to our delegates and others with smart phones, we saw the heartbreaking truth. Seth Rich was murdered. Julian Assange and WikiLeaks published the DNC emails and the John Podesta emails.

Social media lends itself to an inordinate amount of nonsense. People sometimes let their egos go wild, triggering and talking trash, unfriending and blocking. There were people who managed to overcome the nonsense and help us find our way in discovering and articulating our truth. We found out that our media was lying to us, so we had to become journalists. We learned that our elected officials, our supposed leaders, had sold out to corporations and no longer had our best interests at heart. We needed leaders who could help us get to the truth.

Ruth Oskolkoff helped us wade through the swampiness of our current reality. She does it by posting articles, memes, and quotes from fellow progressives. She is bright and clever and has a knack for finding good content and a great sense of humor. Her one rule is to insist that people be civil to each other on her page. I believe that her one simple rule is what made her Facebook page an oasis in a desert of unmemorable conversations.

Ruth is an excellent writer and poet. When she couldn't find a children's version of the Tao te Ching for her son, she wrote Voyage to the Sun. She has also published a collection of poems, Sacramentals, and a later one, Detained, that is in honor of Julian Assange, who is a hero of our movement.

Ruth and I became Facebook friends in May of 2016. I have never met her in person, but I cherish her friendship and look forward to reading her insightful posts every day. I know that she has a young son and a husband and a job. She lives in an apartment in Seattle and doesn't have a car. I know more about how she spends her days than I do about the friends I lost since 2016. I even know that she does what she does from a phone.

This volume of quotes is a part of history, a part of awakening.

As we talked, we realized that we have common hopes and dreams. We want to be kind to each other and take care of each other. We want everyone to have food and shelter and healthcare. We all want to be valued for our services. We want to honor and protect our planet. We want peace.

We know that there are adequate resources here on earth so that no one should have to do without. We want happiness and fulfillment. We want to be able to explore and develop our skills and talents. We want to learn. We looked at our system of increasingly unregulated capitalism and decided that we'd be better off with democratic socialism. We want fair elections with candidates that are not bought. We want money out of politics. We want our elected officials to be public servants who work for us. We want a different world.

Enjoy the conversation.

Louise S. Lee
Hot Springs, Arkansas
November 20, 2018

PREFACE

This book started with the belief that the average person is as intelligent and insightful as the super-rich or the famous. That all of us are smarter, better, and more talented than the 1% tell us. That we all should run the world - not them. That one of the lies of the ruling class is that some people are special and some are not. Huge lie. Each of us can be magnificent, and the powerful are not better. Rather, they are the ones keeping the world in shambles and death.

So, I started featuring interesting quotes on social media from my online friends. Sharing the words in response to posts on my page. Words that are as sarcastic or funny, witty, heartbreaking, or moving - as much any well-known quote.

Others seemed like this approach, so I began to think of creating a book so that many others can share the wisdom from my friends. I hope you enjoy reading these as much as I have.

Never forget that we the people are as worthwhile as those who run the world. Each of us can be amazing if we are but given the chance. If we are but provided the right conditions. We are, after all, the workers who make the world go around. We are the 99%. We are the ones we have been waiting for. Together we are the best hope for change.

ACKNOWLEDGEMENTS

I acknowledge first and foremost those whom I quote in this book. Your courage is indomitable.

Sneha Sinha whose beautiful art is featured on the cover.

Louise Lee who wrote the foreword and captured the spirit of the progressive movement on social media.

My family who gave up time so I can compile this work.

Thanks to Linda Black Elk and Phil Rockstroh for the title idea present in your unique words.

For all my socialist comrades who work for a better world.

For my countless friends on social media who offer advice and encouragement every day.

EPIGRAPH

A million fireflies dance in my peripheral vision
I must admit the show is worth the price of admission -
I've already forgotten my human condition,
Maybe this is what it feels like to die.

The night sky is wide open and the moon three-quarter size
And it shimmers on the river making shadows in the light,
And the stars and clouds look painted and
This whole scene fills my eyes.

This must be what it feels like to die.

by Barb Moose Carbon, written in Asheville on the
banks of the French Broad on June 16, 2016.

ABBREVIATIONS

1% = The top percent income earners.
99% = The majority of people. Earn less than top incomes.
86'd = Thrown out or asked to leave an establishment.
Antifa = Those who protest fascism.
bc = Because.
BLM = The Black Lives Matter movement.
CEO = Chief Executive Officer who heads corporations.
CO =. Carbon monoxide gas. Toxic.
Co2 = Carbon dioxide gas. Greenhouse gas.
CT = Computed Tomography Scan. Medical procedure.
DAPL = Dakota Access Pipeline.
DemEnter = Strategy to enter the Democratic Party.
DemExit = Strategy to work outside the Democratic Party.
dnc = Democratic National Committee.
FB = Facebook
F-Bomb = Using the word 'Fuck' to shock the audience.
Generation Z = Born 1995 – 2009.
GMO = Genetically modified organism.
hrc = Hillary Rodham Clinton.
Ijs = I'm just saying.
IV = Intravenous therapy. Way to administer medications.
Kaep = Colin Kaepernick. Knelt during national anthem.
kkk = Ku Klux Klan.
KXL = Keystone XL crude oil pipeline.
LGBTQ = Lesbian, gay, bisexual, transgender and queer.
MO = Missouri.
NFL = National Football League.
POC = Person of Color.
ptsd = Post Traumatic Stress Disorder.
RT = Russia Today. News Organization.
TLDR = Too long, didn't read.
TPP = Trans-Pacific Partnership. Defunct trade agreement.
US = United States of America.
VA = Virginia.
WTF = What the fuck! Expression of shock.

Quotes for Gardeners, Lovers, Activists, and Allies

A **friend of ours** died today. He was an activist for humanity. He went to stand with #StandingRock and when he came back, he had what many refer to as the DAPL cough after being exposed to the military grade tear gas used on the protesters there. He suddenly started reacting to medications he had been on for other health reasons and his health declined since. Doctors couldn't seem to explain why this was happening, and now a hero who stood up for my children's future is gone, murdered in slow motion so billionaires could profit. This is a story I'm hearing isn't that uncommon. Bastards.

— Timothy Havener

A **normal average** person doesn't understand politics or the nuances. Talking down to them is the first step one takes to becoming part of the system. The out of touch liberal elites show these qualities in excess. They don't even try to hide the fact that they think the average person is stupid and needs to be told what's best for them. We are all guilty of talking down to people. I know I certainly am. But I try to check myself now.

When you become part of the management, you're not part of the labor; you're a representative of the masters. Your goals are to 'manage' the labor. When you enter bourgeois politics, your goals become about those ideas you used to talk about with a touch of 'Well, realistically...' and voila, you've become what you hated. I know that I've tried explaining to people what's realistic and what's not. And it's true; it's not false.

To get anything done, you have to be realistic about what is possible. Is it possible to end wars? Fuck no. Is it possible to pass a puny amendment about it that does nothing but it makes yourself feel better? Sure.

Let's just be honest about things though- when you switch over to management to get something done, make sure you empower the people to start representing themselves and not begrudge them for making the same demands you did when you were part of labor.

This power hierarchy exists. When you're in power, don't begrudge the powerless who question you. You're answerable to them. Listen to them.

— Tania Singh

American-style democracy gave us Jim Crow; Mass Incarceration; 800 military bases in 70 countries; the present colonization of Puerto Rico, Guam, Virgin Islands, Samoa, Marshall Islands, Palau, Micronesia, and the Northern Mariana Islands; at least 80 coups or coup attempts of other governments since 1954; wealth disparity unequaled in history; countless exploitation; the repression of Black and Indigenous people in the States and throughout the world; and Donald J Fucking Trump.

— Jason Dye

Capitalism Must Be Composted

A **nother** fabricated excuse for going to war...The cycle continues. Vietnam, Iraq, Libya, so many others...All in the name of profit, power, and the expansion of the military industrial complex. While this means nothing coming from me and I am powerless, I am so sorry to the people of Syria. This must end. I will do all I can in my lifetime to make it end. A declaration of war under these circumstances must be considered as a crime against humanity. This is illegal and unauthorized. I wish Syria peace one day.

— Sarah Cecelia

A**s a vegan** socialist, I sometimes struggle with the directive to eat the rich. I mean, I get it, but maybe we could just let them loose in a preserve somewhere where they won't be a danger to anyone?

— Matt Mitchell

As long as we continue to force our own people to drink poisoned water, shoot them down in the streets, deny them a good education, and refuse to give them adequate healthcare, we have NO BUSINESS holding other governments accountable for human rights abuses. We have no credibility whatsoever.

— Ryan Skolnick

As long as we feed the rich our tears in single-use plastic bottles, we HAVE purposeful lives.

— Teresa A. Frene

As **your white** supremacist friends and family work to tear you down - NEVER FORGET - FIRST - they come for the socialists. WHY? Because you can't get to the immigrants and the trade unionists and all the others with all these fucking socialists in the way.

— Julie Hickey

Quotes for Gardeners, Lovers, Activists, and Allies

Ask your doctor if blaming Ambien for your racism is right for you.

— Jake Davis

Attorney General Jeff Sessions wants to once again crack down on marijuana users and I agree. I remember watching Reefer Madness at The Biograph Theater in Chicago, stoned out of my gourd and laughing so hard that I think I twisted something...like permanently.

Please Beauregard, return us to those innocent days of Mint Juleps on the veranda and the uplifting spirituals sung by prison slave labor, toiling in the fields of American greatness. Bless you - you cuddly if misshapen little garden gnome.

— Joseph Jaroch

Quotes for Gardeners, Lovers, Activists, and Allies

B **e the change** you want to see in the world, what does that mean? When you open your eyes and the universe looks out do you want it to see a cold, dark place full of paranoia and fear? Or do you want it to see the warm glow of love, a magical, mystical inviting place where dreams come true?

This year I decided to stop making my decisions based on fear and start making them based on love. I quit living a life I didn't love simply because I was afraid I couldn't get anything better and something amazing happened when I did that; I stopped being afraid. I ran for National Delegate for Bernie Sanders and I absolutely loved it, I met the most amazing people and I love them; and they love me right back. I booked a reunion show for my long defunct band so I could bring us together again and do what we love, and we're doing it. I'm now living a life I love because I turned off the fear, and that reaches all areas.

You can't get me to vote for hrc because donald is scarier; i'm not afraid of either of them. I'm not saying stick your head in the sand, i'm not. I'm working for a better world for everyone I love, and I can only take responsibility for myself. I love taking that responsibility on. Be the change you want to see in the world, here's my advice: Love, love deep, love hard, make love, all you need is love, love your life, love your body, love somebody else's body, love your family, love your neighbors, love the fact that life is a struggle and nothing is perfect, love winning, love the lessons you learn when you fail.

Turn off the fear, no one gets out alive; and love that fact too. The fact that we're mortal makes spending time with people you love the most important thing there is. There's a wonderful world with wonderful people out there, love it. With all this talk of love, is it possible I could be in love??? Hmmmmmmm, Let's just say there's a beautiful friction.

— William Barker

B eing 'woke' is not fucking cool. It is a very raw experience with reality. Whatever layer of truth you're digging through, realize that when you keep going, you'll reach a point where it gets really uncomfortable. Keep going. You'll start to feel anger confusion and sense of betrayal. Everything you see changes. The filter comes off and the real ugliness of a class-based rigged world economy you'll never be able to just vote away comes into view.

Keep going.

Hopelessness will try to filter in with a taint of self-interested pragmatism. Keep going. You realize all of your efforts for organized charity are basically empty gestures used to gaslight any real change and rob the rest of us of our outrage. Keep going. You begin to understand that change happens one person at a time. In fact, all change happens this way: One little piece at a time until you reach a critical mass.

Keep going...

— Timothy Havener

Between corporate demons like Nestle and Monsanto, the very right to life itself is becoming a commodity with a price tag as access to food and water become a privilege only available to those who have the means to pay for it.

— Fred Sullivan

Both parties see the citizenry as an annoyance in the way of their mission to extract all profit out of every single thing on the earth that has value.

— Mathew Leutwyler

Capitalism Must Be Composted

C **apitalism is a god** that has failed. The system, based on ever increasing profit margins, has all but killed the oceans of the earth, is rapidly destroying the viability of weather systems crucial to sustaining human existence e.g., the utter disruption of Gulf Stream currents responsible for engendering seasonal changes; the massive release of methane gases by fracking and the warming of the planets polar regions…is creating a feedback loop that will change the ecological systems of the planet to such a degree that will bring on human extinction e.g., 70 percent of the insect population of the planet has simply vanished.

Moreover, the system has created such vast wealth inequity that the political class is wholly owned and controlled by the economic elite thereby making meaningful change impossible. The essence of the fantasy-reeking belief system of capitalists: 'The genius of the free market will find a path forward.'

Reality: The path forward entails this reality: capitalism must be composted, rotten root to noxious fruit. Why? The system, due to its inherent, vast wealth inequity allows the hyper-predators of the economic elite to own and control both the political class and monopolize cultural criteria.

Moreover, are you joking or simply delusional by insisting that the internet is responsible for climate chaos, the acidification of the world's oceans, methane feed-back loops, the disruption of the Gulf

Stream...when the main culprits are factory farming and corporate controlled agricultural practices, the emissions of a system of global-wide jet travel, the obscenity of fracking, and an economic paradigm based on fossil fuels in general.

Finally, you are advised to cease getting high by compulsive Ayn Rand panty sniffing and waiting for Free Market Jesus to descend and walk the earth and lay hands on the earth's dying ecosystem. The hackwork figure of the John Galt character is straight out of a bodice ripping romance fantasy. Genre-wise, we are confronted with the gangsterism inherent to capitalism.

— Phil Rockstroh

Capitalism Must Be Composted

Capitalism is inevitably directed by psychopaths. We are in late stage capitalism, when this becomes most apparent, guised only by censorship before the collapse. Become more informed or be part of the problem.

— Ruth Allen

D **ear peaceful citizens** of the world. My country, The United States, is currently being taken over in a coup d'état on all fronts by the wealthiest class, and the large corporations. The people have lost all power. Please help. The entire world is threatened by these greedy, heartless, power-hungry monsters.

— Michael Anthony

Donald Trump signed my death certificate this morning. If the assistance I get for the two medications that keep me alive goes away, I will die because I cannot afford to pay $2,000 a month. So, I'm going to plan my own funeral next week. I don't want a wake or a death notice or a Mass. Just fry me and drop me in the grave I purchased already. I never thought one man could kill me with the stroke of a pen, but it happened this morning by this heartless bastard. It's been a good run beating the odds for many years with two life-threatening illnesses, but now I'm preparing myself mentally to die.

— Joe Predmore

Even though I'm constantly encouraged to be outraged I will not denigrate other people due to their opinions or beliefs. I will continue to engage people of differing opinions as my equals, and will not assume that because their opinions are different than mine, that they are any less intelligent, more privileged, or just dolts. We have to communicate with each other, we have to hang out on the other side of the fence, we have to seek peace with those we perceive to be our enemies. We are the masses!

— J.d. Reeves

Capitalism Must Be Composted

Examples that prove we are living in a contrarian, Orwellian society: A group of ultra-wealthy capitalists' lobbies for and gains the right to spend unlimited money to buy elections and legislation that favors them instead of average citizens, and the group is called 'Citizens United.' WTF? A set of laws that turns a once free society into a surveillance state and limits civil liberties, and the freedom and rights of honest dissenters who really care about national freedom and justice is called 'The Patriot Act.' A private health insurance plan that has slightly lower premiums with high co-pays and deductibles, as well as fines (i.e. extortion) for those who don't pay up is called 'The Affordable Care Act.' A law that allows for the destructive logging of formerly protected National forests is called the 'Healthy Forests Initiative.' Laws that diminish the collective bargaining rights of workers are called 'Right To Work' laws (Journalist Thom Hartmann states that it should really be called the 'Right To Work For Less' Act).

— Michael Anthony

F **or the love** of God, humanity and all the good things in this world, please, let's look deeper than what the government is showing us on the surface. Trump has been a ridiculous failure as a president and leader of one of the greatest countries in the world. This is history replaying itself. Nuclear Threats bouncing back and forth from North Korea. Bush did this same thing with Iraq. He created a war to save his ass. Trump is about to do the same thing. The only difference is, North Korea really does have weapons of mass destruction. While everyone is running around screaming they're threatening us, all they're really doing is saying, leave us alone, otherwise there will be consequences. It's just like a dog barking at you and warning you that it will bite you. Why does our government want to be that drunk jackass that thinks it can still try petting it or try controlling It? Law enforcement is showing us right now that they don't care if the dog is really friendly or not, they're just going to kill it. That's what our government is doing right now! Come on people, look at more than just the surface. Our government is trying to drown us!

— Guy Scott

F **riend: There** seems to be a perception from people outside of Charlottesville that what is going on here is two opposing groups coming to town and fighting some ideological battle that has gotten messy. That is not what is happening here.

What is happening here is that several hate groups from the extreme right have come together under the 'unite the right' banner here in our town and basically started acting as terrorists. This may seem like an exaggeration but it's not. A church service was held over because they had surrounded the building and police had to disperse them. People had to be escorted to their cars. My friend was there with her daughter. Everywhere they meet, businesses close.

We had drive by shootings yesterday from a van marked kkk. A car plowed into a huge group of people. I'm sure you saw that on the newsfeeds. What you probably didn't see is that some of those people were on their way back from helping to repel a white supremacist march to predominately black housing development a few blocks away where they were attempting home invasions. I guess they were unfamiliar with the neighborhood.

The residents repelled that one before Antifa got there but there is some video of the alt-right folks getting run off on the daily progress twitter feed, if you're interested. So, basically, what I'd like you to understand is, this IS NOT two side egging each

other on to unavoidable violence for more attention. This is one side of terrorists declaring that they can and will hold a town hostage (they've been saying it for over a month now, actually) and the town responding to that threat.

The car that killed and injured people yesterday? Ohio tags. The medic tents, water bottles, snacks, shade tents (all volunteer, donations, none shut down by police... all manned by that radical left you keep hearing about) yeah, we all live here. I saw a lot of people I knew yesterday, none of them were speaking for unite the right. None of them were escalating violence, most of them were offering some kind of aid and defending. I'm glad you're following the situation, but your generalizations are inaccurate in this case. Be blessed.

— Tanya Sheared

G **OING WITH** THE FLOW. When I was kid I used to be a daredevil. My proclivity for danger often exceeded my experience or common sense. One year at summer camp, I snuck off to the river after it had rained and the currents were high. I jumped into the swimming hole shoes and all. I went to swim back to the rock I had just departed when I felt myself being pulled back and down. I struggled for a few minutes treading water and then I went under. I didn't want to, but my body just gave out after fighting the current. Just moments later, one of my cousins happened to be nearby and he jumped into the water and saved me.

In that moment between fighting the unstoppable current and letting go because you can't fight anymore is an allegory for where we find ourselves politically and socially in this country. We're all in with no way back to shore fighting a current of corruption and greed so powerful all we can do is tread water until we go under. No matter what we do, no matter how strong we fight, all our victories are turned to defeat by an insurmountable foe pushing us down with an invisible hand. Free market jokes aside, our political will is barely enough to keep what's left of democracy afloat in America.

Most of us support universal or single payer health care. Most of us want changes to our gun laws, even those who believe in the second amendment. We know things are broken and that our elected officials don't listen to us because they don't have to. Money buys votes and most Americans are broke...yes, yes, I know. The stock market is doing awesome, right? Funny thing that 56% of Americans have less than one thousand dollars to their name.

All that wealth is going to people who already have it. If those tax cuts pass, Donald Trump will make sure they've got even more. The Republicans are so nakedly screwing the American people right now it's hard to watch as poor and middle-class Trump supporters do mental gymnastics that defy natural law to give our current President polling numbers that constantly scrape the bottom of the barrel. The lengths that some on that side of the aisle will go to put their party over people reached a new low with the desperate attempt to whitewash an alleged pedophile from Alabama.

Democrats aren't the shining city on a hill that they want progressives to think they are as much as they are a slightly more left version of a corporate schill as their political counterparts. The double speak recently while they openly admit that the primary was effectively rigged, but the unwillingness to acknowledge the violation perpetrated on voters is nothing short of mental abuse in the form of outright gaslighting.

They are still taking corporate cash and Hillary supporters who helped undermine the 2016 primary are still in power with absolutely no transparency as they lie to our faces and expect the people they defrauded to keep taking it.

Here in the throes of what seems like forces of nature we don't seem to have much choice, do we? Our legs and arms are tired and the rich and powerful are like an unstoppable flood dragging us down. We seem at the mercy of those who can swing elections with just a fraction of their wealth. This is where my comparison ends, and you realize that you have been the victim of an illusion.

The truth they do not want you to see is that they are not the overpowering current, you are...or rather, we are. That force you feel pulling away your hope giving rise to what seems like inevitable surrender is a dream they don't want you to wake up from, because if enough of us ever did we would swallow them whole in one election cycle.

For all their wealth and influence, if just a large portion of citizens decided to unify and rise up for themselves the richest among them would be me in that river fighting an unstoppable force just to try and stay above the water. This is why they spend so much on elections. This is why they try so hard to get you to accept defeat as pragmatism. If you truly achieved together what they fear in their most honest moments of reflection, there would be a cleansing flood that no one could spin back into control.

All you have to do is wake up. All that is required is that you've finally had enough.

— Timothy Havener

G**rowing up** I always thought that being an American meant that we were the protectors, that we were the good guys. That we were a brave melting pot of people that cared about each other and the world we were living in. I thought that police were good guys, the military was for promoting peace and protecting us from harm. I thought that the 'People in charge' were working in our best interest...Man it sucks growing up, and learning the truth. Our children deserve better. My children thankfully are not growing up with the same rose-colored glasses. They are awake in ways that I was not. It is our responsibility to step up and acknowledge that it is time for real change - not the going backwards to the good ol' days kind of change. But real visionary, forward thinking, life changing, (for the good) change. Now is the time for action.

— Tanette Landon

Having been raised in the South, I feel our nation's racism like a broken bone in my own body. When I read To Kill a Mockingbird as a kid, like so many White people, I recognized for the first time the horror of being born into a culture that silently and consistently does violence against People of Color. I realized that I do not have to be actively bigoted to be a White Supremacist, I just need to be a good citizen in that system, and never question why some of us are being left out. In other words, to be popular in any system of oppression costs us our souls.

So, when I heard the NFL owners ruled yesterday that Black athletes will not be free to protest before the symbol of their supposed freedom, and, that during celebrations of our nation's supposed unity, they will not be welcome to express their grief about state violence committed against Communities of Color, I felt the ancient wound. When White people use the flag as an excuse to silence Black protest, I feel the same shudder of horror as when the Klan uses the Christian cross as a symbol of loyalty to the White narrative of our nation's history. It is BECAUSE we love this nation that we must not close our eyes to its history of racism. As long as any one of us is being forced to rise before the symbol of our liberty, every free soul must take a knee.

— Jim Rigby

Capitalism Must Be Composted

Humankind has used race, religion, and nationality to divide us from one another. And, we have allowed capitalism to employ the above to keep us divided and subjugated in the service of the wealthy and powerful predominantly white men. It's time for a change and we must begin by recognizing our commonality rather than focus on our differences. It is time to tell the ruling class to fuck off, your days of exploitation and wars are over.

— Dave Alpert

Humans only succeeded by cooperating with each other. Capitalism unchecked will destroy civilization.

— Carol Mannarino

I am in St Louis. Less than an hour ago yet another white cop was acquitted of murdering a yet another black man. This case was one of the most obvious cases-- the cop was on audiotape saying he was 'going to kill the motherfucker.' The People are already crying...demanding...No Justice No Peace.

— Mary Beth Elderton

I **am proud** to say I Am A Socialist! Although I only became one a few years ago, after many years of trying to reform the Democratic party, and the system, through various liberal methods, such as writing members of congress, making phone calls, trying to buy things based on social responsibility etc... In which I would get back form letters from congress thanking me for my opinion, but that they were of course going to vote the way they wanted to (bought and paid to vote) anyway...I also realized that under capitalism that there was never any real way of buying things responsibly since all things produced under capitalism required some method of exploitation... And seeing that most people like myself who worked hard were not getting anywhere, and many times falling behind, getting further in debt, losing their homes, etc...While those at the top who do not know the meaning of hard work were getting wealthier from the blood and sweat of others...In the US where the system of capitalism is rarely named and exposed, and where the ideas of socialism are kept hidden from public view, it is a miraculous event and exuberant awakening when one comes to call themselves a Socialist.

— Maryann Mcbard

I am the dumbass. a fucked-up poem. i am the dumbass who sat around alone in her room calling hundreds of strangers for months on end begging them to vote for Bernie Sanders... i am the dumbass who spent a weekend in January 2003 driving to and from Washington DC in a fucking ice storm just to spend 6 hours freezing to death to protest the Iraq war in front of the white house right before it happened anyway...i am the dumbass who thinks bitching on social media about politicians who don't give a fuck about me or anyone else will actually change people's opinions or bring real change to this fucked up capitalist system encased in bullshit...i am the dumbass who once upon a time actually thought i could do something to change this stupid, pointless world.

— Lorraine Phillips

I came really close to giving up on the human race last night. I almost succumbed to that 'we are fucked' attitude that I see creeping in on so many people in the United States and beyond. Last night I thought about everything that's going on: war with North Korea, flooding in Houston, Savannah Graywind, HolyElk Lafferty's sister...Cheyenne Rose, King Cheeto's reign of terror, pipelines, uranium mines, tar sands, fracking, genetically modified salmon escaping into the wild, inedible food, unbreathable air, dead soil, undrinkable water, the collapse of bee colonies, genocidal oil magnates...yeah...I could go on. I've heard a lot of people say that they don't want to bring children into this crazy world.

But last night, as I was feeling hopeless and full of tears, I looked at my children and realized that they are everything I have ever hoped for...and I suddenly remembered that everything good in this world is inside of them. How could I ever second-guess my responsibility in making this world a bit better for them before I leave? How could I ever doubt their ability to make this world amazing and beautiful after I am gone? And then I thought about all of you and your children...I thought about the water protectors, the pipeline fighters, the strong men & women who are standing up for the sacredness of women everywhere, the gardeners, the lovers, the activists, allies, artists, singers, dancers, and writers...the foragers and the healers who walk with me on the prairie as we eat sun-ripened berries and make good medicine for the people.

I remembered all the people who dream about an amazing future for our people and our Mother Earth...and I took a deep breath and realized that the world is beautiful and I'm so happy to be here.

— Linda Black Elk

I don't know about you guys but I am so thankful platforms like Facebook and YouTube censor and remove content for us. I trust they have my best interest in mind. Made me feel so good to scroll through my YouTube subscriptions and see so many channels taken down. Who needs alternate versions of anything when we'll be provided the best version of the truth by these benevolent corporations. We should all be thanking them.

— Kate Chapman

I don't know guys, I kind of feel like we already heard the Nazis/White Supremacists out and gave them a chance to express their beliefs 80 years ago when we fought a war over who's ideals were right, 60 million people died, and then we brought the rest of the Nazi leaders to trial in Nuremberg. We didn't say 'well they're entitled to their opinion I suppose.' We sentenced them all to death and hung them. Nazi symbolism and the Swastika have been outlawed in Germany ever since. In the news today, I saw that a drunken American tourist in Germany gave the Nazi salute in a bar last night and German citizens beat the shit out of him. I think the consideration over whether they deserve to be heard or not is long past.

— Mike Canada

I had a mostly sleepless night last night. It all started at 11 pm last night when I got the notification the tax bill passed. I couldn't stop thinking about how this is really going to change things. I thought about my parents who are retired and on Medicare. I thought about my brother who I spoke of earlier in the week. He has lots of medications he takes and needs to be in a group home for supervision. I thought of a lot of people that need a hand up rather than a hand out (that's how I say it). Many programs will be cut so that we can give tax breaks to the wealthiest Americans and American Corporations because they pay WAY too much in taxes.

This country isn't even recognizable to me anymore. I don't know if I can sing the National Anthem, or America the Beautiful, or say The Pledge of Allegiance. I don't believe this country is great. We are involved in conflict around the world that kill civilians for our interests - not to protect them and provide a better life.

Our government is slowly overturning every freedom that made this country great. Getting us addicted to media that propagandizes us daily until we become zombies. We must make sure to stick every one of these passed and even failed bills to the Republicans and even the Corporate Democrats.

We have to take over. I don't know how to do it but I know there isn't much more for them to take from us so what do we have to lose. I want to believe again. I am a bit heartbroken this morning. I still have hope and my wish is you do too. If you feel like me then we must find a way to stand together. What great way to start the Holidays.

— Patrick Conklin

I had a séance, and long story short, Nixon wants to know how many smashed hard drives equals 18 minutes of erased audio tape?

— Michelle Bush

I **keep hearing** people in the establishment media, and people being interviewed by people in the establishment media, and people who rely on establishment media for the truth, express concern about RT America being 'state-sponsored media.' This concern is interesting. The people who have shows on RT America are some of our finest journalists, thinkers, and comedians. They are among our bravest, most outspoken citizens. They represent some of the best that America has to offer in their professional fields, independent-thinking individualists willing to get outside of the box and who take their place as high-profile members of their fields very seriously. If establishment media would allow them to have their shows on US networks, American viewers would watch them. The ones who DID have their shows on major networks WERE watched and appreciated by their audiences for their willingness to speak truth to power.

These Americans who were banned from US corporate media and forced to take their messages to RT America did not break any laws, did not violate any codes of ethics, did not offend any audiences. They were banned because the billionaires who own establishment media, and the powerful industries that spend millions of advertising dollars on establishment media, don't want their audiences to hear what these people have to say, because what they have to say is inconsistent with the financial interests of these billionaire owners and their powerful advertisers. Anyone who supports this censorship of dissenting voices within our media are the ones who concern me. When they engage in red-baiting by calling these Americans with shows on RT America, and those of us who watch them, 'communists' and 'Putin puppets,' when they attack RT America as 'state-sponsored media,' while demonstrating over and over again how misinformed they are about world events - a level of misinformation that is directly linked to their choosing to get their news solely from US corporate media sources, which is not really news at all but rather has become very disturbing propaganda combined with avoidance of controversial topics - they answer the question from 20th century history that we've been asking since the end of World War II - How could the German people have allowed their government to commit the atrocities they did?

Those of us who are awake to the reality of what our corporate-sponsored media represents, now have the answer to that question which my generation - baby boomers - has been asking since I was in elementary school in the 1950s and 60s. Now we have a better idea of how Hitler came to power and was able to do what he did. We're watching how it happens. When I read the comments by these red-baiters, I am both enraged and saddened.

But I am also hopeful, because today we are more awake and connected with others who are awake, so we know we're not alone in being on the right side of this historic moment in US history. And we're not afraid, like so many in Germany were, to speak out, because we are connected now.

There will undoubtedly be an effort to shut down our ability to connect. But they will not be able to do this. Ever. And we KNOW that those who are attacking us with their red-baiting stupidity will have some answering to do to their grandchildren and great grandchildren at some point, about their positions today, and why they didn't step up to the challenges we face with our own corporate-sponsored media, which has done so much to promote international conflict and done so little to rally the troops to address climate change.

Shame on those who engage in this red-baiting. And viva all the outstanding shows on RT America that SHOULD be on US corporate-sponsored networks. The people who host those shows are heroes during a time when heroes in the media are a rarity. I understand why Rachel Maddow does what she does - $30,000 a day, that's why. But those who buy that red-baiting without her paycheck to go along with it? I don't understand them, but I do know they're wrong. And one day, they will know they're wrong, too.

— Linda Carpenter Sexauer

I **know a lot** of folks are celebrating Kaep for being the hammer that broke the dam of the NFL and broad cultural silence on racist police brutality AND I stand right alongside everyone in doing so. BUT I want to take a moment to celebrate those of us thousands and thousands of activists and ordinary people who came out for BLM actions in the years prior and helped forge the hammer that Kaep was able to make use of. Hat tip and black power fist to all of us who marched, sat in, shouted, chanted and loudly proclaimed Black Lives Matter(TOO)! NOW, for something even more important - Let's make this wonderful gushing of solidarity pay concrete dividends - let's start locking up killer cops for lengthy sentences and establish elected independent civilian control boards with full powers over police. Let's build mass organized multiracial movements to give victorious battle to the racist capitalist institutions, dismantle them and build something worthy of humanity!

— Teddy Shibabaw

I know Bernie woke us up in many ways. He taught me a lot. I'm catching a lot of flak for applying it. However, when I think about it - Julian Assange is my biggest hero. He shone light in the dark places where people are still afraid to go. I will not vote for the lesser evil. I will not vote in fear. War is evil. Dems don't stand against it. THAT makes them for it. Nuff said.

— Debra Petton Bell

I raised six wonderful independent children on a meager paycheck. I worked long hours, picked through people's garbage, took hand me downs from anyone willing to share, had no health care insurance and paid for everything over the course of my life. I never went bankrupt or hurt anyone financially, or in any other way. Life has always been a struggle. Just like my parent's life. My kids are already feeling the financial pain of our elite structured society. We need to end this cycle. Our financial situations do not change from generation to generation. Only the lie changes. The elite have taken complete control and use the media and their puppets to make us believe change is coming. It isn't. Not Trump, not Clinton, not Sanders, or any other politician will ever change the system we are now by law, forced to live in. We need to revolt en mass. Every person; race, creed, religion, belief, sexual orientation, political affiliation, financial status, no matter who or where you are in life, need to come together and rid our country of the elite parasitic greedy scumbags that have built their empires on our naivety. We are only as free as their laws allow.

— Mike Wright

Capitalism Must Be Composted

I read on my wall of an American friend who had a hospital stay which, thanks to really good insurance, only cost her a few hundred bucks. I stayed in the hospital for 3 days. I had an X-ray, an Ultrasound, and will end up having 3 CT Scans. I had several meals, I got a leg brace, IV, pain meds including morphine, several consultations with an Orthopedic surgeon, several others with an Orthopedic resident...And I paid 20 bucks for the prescriptions they sent home with me. That's it. I wish with all my heart that no one - NO ONE has to choose between their health and their rent. Or their health and feeding their children. It's horrific that this is happening in the richest country in the world.

— Elizabeth Collins, a Canadian

I **really don't** give a shit if you DemEnter or DemExit. We got to help each other in either circumstance when the time comes.

— Tania Singh

I think #metoo is the final straw in accepting, unconditionally, anyone's right to assume domination over anyone from a point of privilege. Now, money and power are losing their strongholds... a ways to go, but any movement that empowers someone to speak up for themselves and unburden themselves with shame and guilt for being put in THAT situation has to have SOME level of resistance from folks who see no wrong in what they should have recognized as bullying since grade school. We are on the right path.

— Teresa Frene

I **think most** of the statues of Confederate soldiers and generals should be melted down and recast into statues of suffragettes, civil rights leaders, scientists, philosophers, and maybe a few velociraptors... we'll hide those in bushes in parks just for the hell of it.

— Andrew Boheler

I try to maintain a balance when it comes to economic issues and racial issues. Like we all can agree racism exists and some of us can recognize it more than others and that's where sometimes the disagreements stem from. Some people see racism in a decision or in a statement and others think that's not racism. There's a lot of people like me who can maintain their cultural identity and have leftist ideology.

My leftist ideology is enhanced by revolutionaries who share the same cultural identity as me. This 'leftist movement is white' issue annoys me to no end. I feel that my identity as a leftist is erased by the mainstream because I'm Indian. How dare any centrists/neoliberals claim that BECAUSE I'm Indian, I should care more about culture than economics. How dare they levy charges of racism against everyone who is fighting for economic justice for all!

Now, I do need some progressives to do better on race issues too. When a person of color tells you they're experiencing racism, believe their experiences. Please. But don't let them gaslight you for not supporting their neoliberal heroes. See? Balance. Now coming to electoral politics, I always go with principles over someone who shares the same cultural identity as me. In fact, I feel, to be successful in politics, poc and women have had to compromise their ideals more and they've been taken advantage of by neoliberals and neoliberals fetishize politicians by their identity and market it to garner support from the masses. It's the worst.

I was even told- you're a woman, you're brown, you're an immigrant, you're perfect for California politics. Well what about who I am on the inside and my ideology? Is California ready for a leftist? Anyways, we can simultaneously call out racist behavior and systemic oppression of poc AND be economically progressive for all. Question motives. Question everything packaged perfectly. Question everything they're selling to you. Let your leftist brothers and sisters of colors correct you if they think you're wrong on something. Don't get defensive. We have the same goals, just different experiences. Believe their experiences and pain too.

— Tania Singh

Capitalism Must Be Composted

I **was going** to make a nice post about Juneteenth, but Nooooo. Those damn police in Seattle made sure there was another thing we need to talk about today. Charleena Lyles (say her name). Called for help because she was being robbed; cops arrived and shot her dead. A story was leaked that she was 'brandishing a knife;' even if she fucking was holding a knife, why didn't Brave Police Cops assume that the knife was meant to scare off burglars? EVEN IF SHE WAS, (which I doubt), why shoot her? Weren't these brave public servants trained enough in de-escalation that they would have just shouted 'drop the knife' (DON'T come on this post and tell me they did that, because they DIDN'T).

The conversation around Ms. Lyles death will probably move towards mental health; fine, good, but let's talk about the mental health of the officers who shot a person calling for help, instead of looking for anecdotal evidence of Ms. Lyle's infirmity so we can neatly blame it all on her. No, I want to know who hurt Officer Pisspants so bad that he had to shoot a woman dead out of blind fear or rage or whatever drove him to pump bullets into a mother standing in front of her children.

Don't tell me, 'we need video evidence of what happened before we know if it was justified.' Spoiler alert: it was not justified. In cases where we do have video (Philando Castile, Eric Garner) it never matters; it's still always the fault of the person in brown skin, never the person in blue khakis. If there was a video, and it showed Charleena Lyles behaving like anyone else would if they were being robbed (up until the point when she was brutally murdered), what then? Your boy will still keep his job, catch no charges; this murder was state sanctioned.

I'm sick of this. Seems like every day, and it also seems like when I express myself along these lines, someone always shows up to tell me that I'm wrong. 'not all cops,' 'we need a video of the incident,' 'they were acting according to their training and duty.' Nope, nope, and nope. There's no denying the terrible reality anymore, y'all, and those that try just look foolish and cruel.

— Stephanie Brown

I **am a bit** late chiming in about the cop who was acquitted of murdering Philando Castile, I know, but I am going to add my thoughts anyway. I watched the newly released dashcam video several times, along with Diamond Reynolds' video, which I have seen several times as well. We have two different videos to watch and put all together as best as possible.

Never did I see a reason to pull a gun on him, let alone shoot him. He was killed because the cop was scared of him, but why? He was killed because of his skintone. The officer had asked for Philando's ID and insurance card, that was what Philando was getting for the cop. He made it absolutely clear he had a firearm. If he was intending to do any harm he wouldn't have told the cop he had a gun.

This makes me so sick to the stomach. We are sending a message to cops that it's OK to be scared of someone who is black, and hell, it is apparently 'self-defense' if you kill them because you are scared. And what gets me, what shakes me to the core, is that Diamond complied and even called the cop 'sir.' She remained calm. She had just witnessed her boyfriend get shot SEVEN times, her child was in the back seat. Yet she remained calm, compliant and respectful. She remembered her training, so why couldn't the officer?

And that sweet baby girl who has undoubtedly been traumatized. She tells her mom to cooperate so she wouldn't get shot. She was 4 when she saw this horrific event. I hope she is doing okay.

— Amy Austin Dunham

I **am about** to do a major rant, filled with lots of F-Bombs. So, if the F-bomb offends you, I apologize in advance and afford you the opportunity to skip what I have to say and pass on by to the next post. Now with that said, here goes!

/////////////// Warning! F-Bomb Material ///////////////

I've had it with these so-called elite motherfuckers! If they're worried about my 'political beliefs,' then have a dose of this! The fucking so-called elites spray the air we breathe as if we were cockroaches. They steal our kids and throw them in prisons or put uniforms on them for war. They pollute our air, land and water and watch us die. They pit us against each other over such fucking bullshit just so they can keep us divided. They make us fight, scratch and claw for every fucking penny for survival while they sit in their ivory towers, drinking out of crystal glasses, behind pearl necklaces. They finance both sides of wars and make the losing side pay off the winning side.

They bomb innocent people who have no fucking idea why they are being bombed! They pit Jews against Arabs, blacks against whites, left against right, men against women, and any other group you can think of. They lie to us in the media. They brainwash you from the moment you become conscious in life. They distract us with garbage and keep us in fear. They know that fear causes us to remain uncertain, immobilized, and seeking their fucking help! They devalue our currency year after year, while decreasing our wages. They keep us enslaved to our shitty jobs, knowing full well that we are living paycheck-to-paycheck and fearing loss of our jobs and basic needs.

They give us pretend elections knowing damn well that they have already chosen the candidates, and in many cases the winner. You are just thinking you are voting. You are voting for shit! They strip us of our jobs, send it overseas, and then call us lazy for not working! They raise the prices of organic foods and feed us GMO garbage that is killing us! They spy on us, sell our personal information to people that do not have our best interest at heart, and censor us if we step out of line.

They do not listen to the majority of the people when we say 'NO.' They just fucking do what they want. They start their imperialistic wars all around the world and expect our children to die for it. Our children come home fucked up in the head, or maimed or worse yet, dead! They let our veterans, that helped them land their big fucking oil bonanzas, go homeless or without help. They put poison into our children's veins and food. They kill our insects and marine life, with pesticides and nuclear contamination. They fucking treat us like lab rats, giving us stimuli and measuring our responses. Rent keeps going up, food prices increase, taxes go up, tuition cost keep rising, but we need to remain civil.

They keep poking sticks at countries, waiting for those countries to respond so that they can then be crushed! I'm so fucking sick of that! They love to get us all riled up in nationalism, while they bankroll both sides of future warring adversaries. Anyway, my rant is over. I'm sure there are a hundred other examples I could have used, but I can't because I'm fucking pissed. I'm getting older and life is getting harder. I sometimes truly believe they are trying to kill us all. The elites would love to reduce our numbers in masse so that they can then control us better. How about we reduce their numbers so that we can control ourselves? That sounds like a great fucking idea! Any of you that want to unfriend, have at it. I don't think anything I've said is untrue. Later I might go down the rabbit hole. What have I got to lose? America, 'land of the brave' has become 'land of the fearful cowards!'

— Joseph Gonzalez

I am really disgusted with the fact that our elected officials can keep details of proposed legislation secret and still force congressmen and senators that haven't seen the legislation to vote on it. The first time I can remember this happening was with Obama's TPP. You would think that there would be a procedure that would guarantee legislators have a month or two to review the details of the laws they are expected to approve. Not only is there no time to read the proposed law, there's no time given to allow lawyers or any experts the time to review the proposed law. How can this be legal? I guess it's the path that dictators take who are in positions of power in a false democracy. They need to continue the illusion that democracy still exists here.

— Angela Basta

Capitalism Must Be Composted

I have noticed how some people consider confrontation to be an inherently negative thing, usually because they claim to value peace. But if my life has taught me anything, it's that the worst violence always hides in the shadows of silence - in the form of excluding, shunning, ignoring, etc. Injustices only have the potential to be addressed when that violence is brought out into the open.

— Kristoffer Hellén

If you are not part of a radical organization - one that is completely separate from the Democratic Party - please consider joining one as soon as you can. Many are trying to work on transformative projects, and there are limitations due to capacity. With more folks involved, the unlikely becomes more likely, and eventually, inevitable. It's not easy. Personality clashes are frequent. It can be frustrating. We are human, you know? But ultimately, it's incredibly rewarding and, in my opinion, worth every second. Thank you!

— Mimi Soltysik

If you listen closely you can hear the sound of the oligarchy firing up its flim flam machine with wings made of propaganda and gears greased with foreign monetary donations.

— Jennifer Gilder

If you think that Homelessness is just about physically striving to stay alive, just take a moment to think of Your Mind, the crushing boredom, the psychological impact of all those accusing eyes, those cursing stares from those who despise people who just need a little kindness, a little heartfelt help. A book or sleep can only offer a fractional relief, an illusion of escape. The harsh reality is always being out there.

— Bryant King

If you want 'unity,' and if you want to defeat Trump, let people like Kshama Sawant, Jill Stein, and Tulsi Gabbard speak. We need them. We need their voices. By silencing them, you are silencing the voice of the people for they speak for many of us. When you choose to not 'approve' them, you choose to not approve us.

— Frantz Pierre

If you want to live in a society without a class system, with free health care, education and housing, a society where everyone is entitled to a job and their human rights, a society where there are no mega-corporations hoarding wealth, where every voice matters, not just the voices of elected politicians...then you're a communist. When we normalize the word communist we can start to see progress. Y'all aren't gonna live in a society with all the things you know every human should be entitled to if you're afraid to even say the word.

— Lola Sankara

In my experience, you get Trump supporters on your side not by endlessly denouncing their leader, but by showing them you share their goal of defeating the Deep State. If we reach out to them in this way, they'll more willingly listen to our criticisms of Trump, and maybe give up the hostility toward people of certain races and religions that demagogues have gotten them to have. I urge everyone to think of this in future interactions with Trump voters.

— Rainer Shea

In **Rome**, there was a senator who ended every speech with: 'Carthage must be destroyed.' We need someone who ends every speech with: 'Flint still doesn't have clean water!' #waterislife

— Cullen Tiernan

Capitalism Must Be Composted

In today's political landscape, political power works by a person not giving in to the lesser evil strategy. As long as they know that you will buy into their coercion of the lesser evil voting strategy, you will never have any political power. You will just find your interests being betrayed over and over and over and further and further and further as you give up all your political power to the corporate elites who control politics right now. The very first and most urgent thing to do is to stop voting for the lesser evil. Don't worry about who else is going to do that, just start doing it yourself. Vote for the candidate that represents your interests and values. Support candidates who do no matter what party or non-party. I believe there is a wave of this starting to sweep the political landscape.

— Laurie Lambe

Instead of every man for himself and all of us scrambling to get to the top, why would it be such a bad thing to pool our resources to make everything better for all of society? I'll just never understand.

— Elizabeth Schultz

Capitalism Must Be Composted

It is the truth. We never saw it coming till we got slapped in the face with it. I am not putting my hope and faith in Bernie Sanders, nor do I hate him. Thankfully he helped me open my eyes and helped me to understand why we live the way we do. For the last 35 years I could see life getting worse and worse, but could not understand why. Now I get it. The Democrats and Republicans, alike, have no use for we the people. I never dreamed my party would turn against me. They are my peers, flesh and blood, and humane, just like me. Boy was I wrong.

— Sharon Pantenburg

It must never be forgotten that, when our nation's founders said, 'We the People,' they meant 'We, the Propertied White Men.' Until liberals and conservatives alike realize that the system itself was built around a rich white male narrative, we will treat prejudice as a personal flaw and not as a cataract in the national vision. We must build a new republic where 'We the People,' truly includes those who are not propertied, white, nor male.

— Jim Rigby

Capitalism Must Be Composted

I t is simple really. I'm an average person ... much like everyone I know. I'm not a murderer. I'm not a thief. I don't lie. I don't cheat. I'm not greedy. I have empathy. I'm not a racist. I don't bully. I love all animals ... wildlife. I don't litter. I conserve my use of water. I garden for food and the bees. I think healthcare is a human right. I believe in unionized work for a safe workplace, appropriate pay and voice in all that effects the employed. I believe in a public and free education for all. I believe in clean safe public drinking water. I do not want anyone spraying anything in my sky. I do not want oil drilling in the oceans, on land, anywhere there is life. I believe in green energy or none at all. I don't want fake food being sold. I want to know where my food is from. I don't want Monsanto, Bayer, any chemical corporation to have anything to do with food production. I don't want my phone to be a spy and tracking device.

I don't want the police killing unarmed and innocent people. I don't want militarized 'public defenders' intimidating and attacking peaceful citizens. I don't want crooked bankers bailed out with Trillions of dollars. I don't believe the poor should be treated as criminals. I don't believe there should be hunger and starvation anywhere. I don't want anyone homeless. I don't think there should be millions of empty houses while fellow citizens are beaten, freezing, etc. with no safe place. I don't want nuclear plants boiling water for electricity. I don't want males dictating laws regarding women's rights referencing reproduction, what is rape, what she wears, etc. I don't want the public airwaves used for state propaganda. I don't want 'news' programs to lie and entertain on behalf of corporate funders. I don't want millions of human beings either murdered, displaced, seeking refuge from terror, made refugees ... All to no fault of their own. I don't think sea life should ever see plastic in their home habitat ... much less die from it. I think that the seriously Disturbed (sociopaths, psychopaths, malignant narcissists, etc.) should be institutionalized for treatment ... Not running the country and businesses. I think that multimillionaire preachers with mega churches should be heavily taxed. I think droning people is an act of Terrorism and immoral and should be illegal. ... there's so much more. Every day I'm made aware of yet another act of INHUMANITY. It's simple really. In my country ... those who rule are in Opposition to all that I am, believe or feel.

— Barbara Hatfield

Jesus **was** the unwanted, the marginalized, the poor, the dirty, the homeless, and the hated folks. He was one who said to protect ALL of your fellow human beings - to do unto others as you would have them do unto you, and to NEVER, EVER judge, until you truly walk in another's shoes. And if you read the Bible or know any of this history, you KNOW this. The vast majority of people who dare call themselves 'Christian' and are highlighted in the media these days are hypocrites. (Just like establishment republicans and democrats are incredible, and incredibly shameless - hypocrites.)

Jesus was a radical. He challenged the toxic, broken, criminal, cruel status quo. He stood up to ALL people and ALL straying from non-judgment, compassion, and genuine brotherhood (and sisterhood), and basic decency and regard, across all differences. He stood up to EVERYTHING we small and terrified human beings come up with, lunge toward, and self-righteously cling to, with our tiny egos. He asked us to do better. He asked us to leap off metaphorical cliff after cliff, to become closer to god. To the all. To embodied, infinite love and compassion. As close as we can get, while in our fallible brains and temporal bodies.

Whether you're Christian or not, it's not a bad message to get behind. It has nothing to do with labels, mega churches, saying 'Merry Christmas' or not, or with whether you want gay people to get married or not; it has even less to do with establishment republicans or establishment democrats - who are all selling us ALL down the river to their actual masters and highest bidders. Jesus was a revolutionary, at the end of the day. He asked more of us than anyone has, save for perhaps the Buddha and Mohammed, Rumi, or Mirabai. He asked us for the hardest revolution possible - one that happens first on the inside, and then amongst us all.

He also spoke of standing up to usury, which is the very shape of our existence these days, making too many of us so fatigued we cannot even think of defending ourselves against and correcting what is happening. All of this is a revolution I can get behind. First on the inside, in every minute and every way possible, no matter how scary or hard. Then, on the outside, in our broken, beleaguered world. And I don't care if you are democrat or republican. If you are suffering, if you are struggling, if you are scared, we are on the same side. It's time to be intrepid enough to see this, so that we can come together, to change our world.

— Tangerine Bolen

Capitalism Must Be Composted

Kamala Harris and the dnc need our help. They have 3 short years to win over progressives by accusing us of being sexist and racist for rejecting yet another corporatist warmonger. We have to get our shit together and compromise our values so that a corrupt party that openly cheats their own constituents can win the presidency and keep the corporatist war machine rolling.

— Maurice Yo

Land. Food. Medicine. Music. Arts. Housing. Literature. Water. Technology. Education. Retirement. Travel. Leisure. And so much more. The world is trapped behind a paywall, waiting to be released.

— Whitney Kahn

Learn to love your master. Your teacher is always right. Your job as a student is to do what you are told. Fall in line bitch.

— Sam Michael

L et's talk about how people are being arrested for feeding the homeless, but the abundance of empty homes. Let's talk about the lack of clean drinking water, but the abundance of oil. Let's talk about all the bloodshed of war, but no policies to help refugees/immigrants. Let's talk about how the US empire was built off the backs of black slaves, but they haven't seen a damn bit of reparations and it's too 'touchy' of a subject to talk about. Let's talk about the colonization of Puerto Rico, but god forbid they'd be allowed to have actual rights, even though they send their children to die in wars for the US empire. Let's talk about how corrupt US politicians use the resources of other countries for their own financial gain, but are nowhere to be found in time of humanitarian crisis. Let's talk about what needs to be done and do it.

— Stevie Eevee

Capitalism Must Be Composted

Life under capitalism is a never-ending state of impending doom. Housing, rent, climate change, war, the police, unemployment (or the threat of unemployment), debt, bigotry, safety, hunger. That's not life. Life under capitalism is violence.

— Mimi Soltysik

Making profit from human misery is the New American Dream.

— Adrian Matthews

More specifically, Work to end gender oppression of female and LGBTQ fellow workers and do not tolerate it in the movement. Work to end White supremacy and do not tolerate it in the movement. Defend your immigrant fellow workers, whether documented or not, and do not tolerate anti-immigrant bigotry within the movement. This is not 'identity politics.' This is REAL working-class solidarity. Those who say 'It's all about class' as a way to ERASE these issues are counter-revolutionaries and should be treated accordingly.

— Lee Einer

M **ost people** spend their whole lives seeking only the ability to live in comfort. That's the American dream after all. Others live to fight without fear, to love without logic, to dance on the edge of mountains and to cry with the deepness of the oceans. The highs and lows of truly living are too much for those who only seek personal comfort. We can choose to live outside of the box. We can climb to the top of the mountain, only to fall from its peaks and begin again. In doing so, we will feel the summit winds and the rocky bottom and we will survive them all. The world will never be changed by those who found their comfort. It will be changed by the ones crazy enough not to seek it in the first place. My friend was kicked out of Boston's South Station last night again for feeding the homeless. All of the cops except 2 said he was doing the right thing and that it was wrong to kick him out. But out he went anyway.

— Chelsea Lyons

My last thought of today is - don't expect neoliberals/Dem elite to ever understand. They go to Ivy League schools and are trained to think they're superior than the masses. Their elitist schooling and upbringing makes them practically incapable of seeing things how we see them. This includes all races. The liberal elites hate Bernie because they see him as completely clueless. The laud him for his integrity but consider him a fool just like they have for 40 years. Lucky for us he kept doing the same thing for 40 years. These elite are groomed to become our leaders because the elite class can never trust the masses to make their own decisions which is why they have superdelegates. We are all dumb and clueless as far as they're concerned. They consider themselves to be the intellectuals, the brains of the operation of this country while we are the hands and feet. Expecting them to understand us is expecting our brain to crawl out of our cranium and wipe our butts. People ask us why we don't support neoliberals over conservatives. We could and we may have to but we literally have to give up our dignity to do it. They take our dignity away by promising to protect us from the Nazis. They give us shelter but they exploit us in their house. They give us food but they rape us in return. And we are supposed to thank them for protecting us while we are on our knees; Bernie or Bust was just us choosing to die on our feet. Have a good weekend guys.

— Tania Singh

Neoliberals embrace capitalism but just want to make it a little fairer for women, minorities, etc. True progressives realize that we cannot address the most important issues of our day (climate change, perpetual war, extreme inequality, unemployment and low wages, etc.) without fundamentally altering capitalism.

— Beverly Burris

Capitalism Must Be Composted

No **matter who** is President, we always end up continuing a war or getting into a new one. North Korea would be the latest in a long list of countries that both Democratic and Republican Presidents have taken an issue with. War is profitable to the 1% and they are willing to send our loved ones to die for this profit. Civilians and the military of either nation pay the price, never the rich men and women that cause the chaos in the first place. I'm not saying we shouldn't be concerned about North Korea's threats, I'm just saying that hasn't everyone realized by now that we are always 'whipped into shape' by our government and media outlets when we start clamoring for change? That we NEED to accept their corruption in exchange for protection from the wars they create? Think about it.

— Tahbarri Clendinen

No TLDR. Life in the modern, capitalist west is tedium. It is an exhausting bore. Without any substantial sense of belonging or meaning, stripped of spirit and tasked with an endless quest for money that buys less and less, people are miserable... The malaise of existence in this world where the wild is all but extinguished is felt far and wide, whether it is understood as such or not. Absent community and a deep sense of both autonomy and personal value, people become damaged... We industrial humans do not live. Living is active. We are only active in the pursuit of making someone else rich while we earn just enough to make it until the next paycheck, and then we are passive.

We sit and stare, trading entertainment for experience, hoping that watching others pretend to live will suffice by proxy... If we all agree to call the cage freedom, then it is freedom. What becomes of people when you strip them of everything that makes them human? ... In my region there are those who want to cut the forests. They think that they have observed the forest long enough to know how to control it. They think they have the wisdom to manage a forest better than it can manage itself.

How does one argue? The only words they will accept are in their own language, the language of domination, the language that insists on seeing only disparate pieces in a grand machine, the language that has exorcized the sacred. I cannot convince you to leave the forest be, in that language. I cannot convince you to seek the wild with those lifeless words. I cannot convince you to abandon this culture in the language that it birthed. You have to feel it. Perhaps you do already. Perhaps you aren't sure what you feel, other than a general sense that something is not right. Do not snuff it out. Nurture it. Breathe life into it. Let it guide you to others. Give yourself permission to feel even if it is only the pain. Move boldly through the darkness, and listen for the howl.

— Mathew Leutwyler

No, no, no. We have lots of freedom here. We have the freedom of speech, the freedom of association, the freedom of movement, the freedom to compete for better junk, the freedom to get beaten up and arrested for speaking, the freedom to be terrorized and murdered for our associations, the freedom to get pulled over and shot to death while we're using our freedom of movement because our killers thought we were a 'suspect' - or maybe just used some bullshit like that as a cover. We have the freedom to get arrested, the freedom to get fined, the freedom to have all of our stuff thrown in the garbage by the cops because we can't afford to pay for storage, the freedom to get 86'd, the freedom to spend our slave-wages on small amounts of deadly and addictive habits that, in effect, take food out of the mouths of our children. We have the freedom to sleep outside with the elements of pollution. We have the freedom to kill ourselves. Etc. Etc. Etc. Lots of freedoms here.

— Evan R. Herzoff

Nobody likes revolutionaries, because we are assholes who punch people in the face, and we have bad language and will bite your fucking face off. But some NICE people will look the other WAY when people go to the GAS CHAMBER.

— Warren Lynch

Quotes for Gardeners, Lovers, Activists, and Allies

Our currency survives only because the dollar now is the only means of oil purchases worldwide, i.e. petrodollar survives because of it and that is why we keep fossil fuel going and not environmentally renewable sources of energy and deny climate change and keep printing worthless money: if it was not for oil! The moment that stops, we invade and crush and that is why we invade countries that drop the dollar as the only means of exchange for oil with the blessings and workings of the central banks. As a wise man once said: 'No currency can hold up in the face of an economy that survives on borrowed money and debt!' Only a strong military can assure that and our military budget dwarfing everyone else's proves that to the detriment of taking care of its own people! You can keep on robbing Peter to pay Paul and keep on going only with the cooperation of both! And that explains why Trump is our president and why we get duopoly choices of evil and less evil every time to choose from in a rigged voting system to help the more evil win and exclude any other party for a corporate owned government and bribed politicians on the take with lobbyist money! All the other things are distractions to keep us divided and fighting and glued to a corporate media for a corporate government robbing us blind in the meantime! And that is a view of today's working of America 101. Sad but so close to the truth with no fog keeping us asleep.

— Stefanos Photiades

People keep asking when will there be a Revolution, and keep waiting for a leader. The answer is the Revolution is now, and the leader is you.

— Lisa Walton

Police were in riot gear at a counter protest of the KKK July 8 in Charlottesville, Va. We brought noise makers like pots and pans and musical instruments; they brought a noisy low flying helicopter, heavy military vehicles, and tear gas. The law forbidding face coverings (intended for the Klan) was used to arrest many protestors who covered their faces after being tear gassed. The police clearly meant to agitate the protestors while protecting the KKK. 23 protestors were arrested.

— Laurel Bosma

Capitalism Must Be Composted

Poverty is essential to capitalism. Severely impoverished workers will take jobs in hazardous environments for low wages. We live in a dark place.

— Susan Nimmo

P **rison labor** means you only have to pay people $10 a month to 'work' for you. The more people that are in jail, the better it is for profits. The highest percentage of people going to jail are minorities -- many times because they are poor and can't afford good legal representation. A lot of times we see them getting longer jail sentences than white people for the exact same crimes (especially if the white person is middle class and has a decent lawyer, i.e. 'white privilege').

For many people in America, it means prison sentences for benign things like possession of weed or mere driving infractions. Nobody should be in jail for simply buying weed. It's ridiculous. But you have to fill up those prisons any way you can. Prison labor is just modern-day slavery. They just call it something different now. Its official name is the 13th Amendment. Now I'm not talking about someone who is serving a life sentence for murder or something equally heinous. I'm talking about the ones that are there for ridiculous reasons. And if you are talking about private prisons, they make money off of people getting thrown into jail. Gotta keep those jails filled to capacity.

Now Wall Street criminals and politicians like Hillary Clinton or George W. Bush (and many others) can commit crimes that damage the entire worldwide economy and/or war crimes, corruption and espionage -- and they almost never face a single day in prison for their massive crimes to humanity.

They are rich and powerful. They are not going to be put to work in prisons anyhow, so they serve the elites no purpose by being there. And they are the elites themselves, so they have the system rigged entirely in their favor. Many of them take money from the private prison lobbies, so they profit off of this corrupt and evil system.

— Jay Mucci

Racism is a serious problem. Charlottesville was a tragedy. Before that everyone was posting about guns after mass shootings, healthcare during the Death Care bill, Russia, Russia, Russia, the 2016 election (relentlessly), DAPL, the list goes on and on and on. AND NOTHING CHANGES. We react to what the media tells us is a crisis and then move on to the next thing the media tells us is a crisis and have a profile pic for every crisis and NOTHING CHANGES. The powers that be don't want anything to change...and we play along. They conditioned us well. We react, then forget, then react...and NOTHING CHANGES.

— Patricia Ruzgis

Recently, **I read** a post on FB insisting that me and my activist friends are in some secret coalition or cabal. Not surprisingly, I've had a few people contact me to ask how to join. Sadly, there is no secret sleeper organization that I belong to. I am a part of a loose collective of people though. You may call us 'The Helpers.' We are the ones that show up to the thing. In fact, we help set up and we are often the last to leave as we help put everything away. By my estimation there is a core group of 15-20 of us that can be counted on to help you do the thing. From fancy charity event to your weekly garden variety protest.

We help sign people into the thing, we help make the signs, we carry the signs, and when it's all said and done we make sure the place is cleaned up for the next people. Some of these folks are Democrats, some are fierce Independents, some are Freethinkers, some are in Indivisible, some have a Honey Pot while others do not, some are a few of those things and more. What we share is an ability to help get things done. Anyone can join and membership is free.

We don't have a secret handshake but I suppose we could add that to the list. We are solution focused and we spend more time doing the thing than pontificating or philosophizing (No blowhards allowed). You will seldom hear us making the speeches or see us leave once the cameras are gone (we see you). - Instead we are the worker bees doing the work. Stuffing envelopes, taking out the trash, running to Costco for the chicken, making that delicious pot of spaghetti that everyone raved about (I see you Janie). We also are the folks that field the complaints and take the flack when things go wrong - as they often do.

We are collaborative, egalitarian and very much woman centered. We eschew classism and all things elitist or oppressive. We have no leader but whoever is best at the thing is often the one in charge of the thing. So, Leadership rotates depending on which hat we are wearing and what the occasion calls for. We share a strong desire to lift of the voices of the oppressed and the marginalized. To join - just show up to the next thing and look for the helpers and repeat this super-secret password 'How can I help you do this thing?' I promise that me, or someone like me, will put you to work.

— Bonnie Kendall

Say what you mean when you say the lesser evil is necessary. You're indirectly saying that as long as the bombs and poverty are kept away from your American doorstep, you're cool with our government terrorizing Africa and the Middle East.

— Tahbarri Clendinen

Shared from a friend who narrowly escaped being mowed down today when a pathetic piece of Nazi scum named James Alex Fields Jr. drove his car into a crowd of anti-racism protesters today in Charlottesville, VA, killing 1 and injuring dozens more:

> *'Was on the street where a car deliberately plowed into a crowd of peaceful protesters. Was barely able to get out of the way but i am ok. I Hope this scum is held responsible for my attempted murder and the attempted murder and vehicular assault of all my comrades. At least one victim is in critical condition and might not make it.*
>
> *Update, One confirmed fatality.'*

— Emily Connor

So, people are not understanding what the NFL players are protesting about the National Anthem. It is the words of the National Anthem stating 'land of the free.' People of color do not experience the level of freedom that white people do. Stop singing a song that DOESN'T represent every human's real experience daily in this country. The National Anthem allows us the feel good about this country that needs much more work! It has NOTHING to do with the brave men and women who have fought for the freedoms we do have. It is all about the complacency that currently exists while members of our communities are being brutalized and murdered by the police. We are NOT the land of the free right now. Our National Anthem currently is a goal not realized and those NFL players are taking a stand and not honoring the song until we are the land of the free for EVERY HUMAN!!!

— Reidun MacGregor

Socialist Suggestion: Don't dress your baby in blue or pink clothing, dress them in red. When someone asks, 'Is it a boy or girl?' You can say, 'It's a comrade.' WIN.

— Fiorella Isabel

Capitalism Must Be Composted

S **omebody asked** when I lost faith in Obama. Well, after voting for him twice, in 2016, he turned his back on the Native Standing Rock Sioux while they were brutalized by Militarized bully Cops and private Oil Pipeline security attacking Peaceful Water Protectors and their children with trained dogs. The DAPL Pipeline moves dirty tar sands oil to the gulf to be shipped overseas! Imagine the carbon pollution this will contribute to the Global Warming crisis. And all Obama could say was, 'Let's see how this plays out.' As Trump prepared to take office. Apparently, they both have money in the DAPL Pipeline. And when he backed Debbie Wasserman Schultz for reelection after the rigged Democratic Primaries. And then I found out he let Citibank choose his entire cabinet! Thanks Wikileaks. Julian Assange, a true hero in a time of very few.

— Alan Grose

Talking with my 14-year-old son...I mentioned the word activist, he asked, 'What EXACTLY is an Activist?'...I gave him a 10-minute explanation. At the end he looked at me and said, 'So someone who is Activated to good for all people fighting corporations, government and social norms, even if those people don't care.'

— Patricia Blanchard

T **hank god** for Julian Assange. Seriously. We wouldn't know s**t without him & WikiLeaks.

— Linda Carpenter Sexauer

THE ABUSER. Face it, progressives are a lot like the victim Charlie Brown. To gain and maintain total control over you, an abuser doesn't 'play fair.' #DonnaBrazile #Superdelegates Abusers use fear, guilt, shame, and intimidation to wear you down and keep you under their thumb. #DemEnter Your first step to breaking free is recognizing that your situation is abusive. #DemocraticPrimary A sign that you may be in an abusive relationship includes a dominant party who belittles you #BernieBros or tries to control you by provoking feelings of helplessness and desperation. #NeverEver You may be told that you should not leave them, that only they can protect you. The aim of the abuse is to chip away at your feelings of independence—leaving you feeling that there's no way out of the relationship. #LesserEvil

They threaten repercussions if you don't do what they want. #Trump Abusers need to feel in charge of the relationship and may treat you like a child. #YoureBeingRidiculous They will tell you what to do, expect you to obey without question and make decisions for you. #DebateSchedule They will say you are powerless without them. #WeAreNotEurope An abuser will make you feel defective in some way, #Spoiler so you're less likely to leave. Insults, name-calling, #Crybabies shaming, and public put-downs are all weapons of abuse designed to make you feel powerless without them. To increase your dependence, an abusive partner will interfere with your ability to communicate and interact with others

freely. #MediaBlackout You need their permission to do things. #FederalElectionCommission The abuser will pressure you to commit to the relationship and make you feel dependent and guilty for wanting to end the relationship. Your abuser may use a variety of intimidation tactics designed to scare you into subordination. They may accuse your allies of being 'trouble makers.' #BernieBullies The clear message is that if you don't comply, there will be serious consequences for you and others.
#TrumpTrumpTrump Denial & blame –Your abuser will minimize their behavior #LikeWithACloth and deny it occurred #AbsolutelyNoClassifiedEmails. Abusers are very good at making excuses for the inexcusable. #ElectionFraud #MediaCollusion They will blame their shortcomings on endless scapegoats, #RussianHackers #DNC #JillStein #Putin and even on the victims of their behavior. #BernieSanders

They will commonly shift the responsibility on to you: Somehow, their misconduct is your fault. And someone is always out to get the abuser or is an obstacle to the abuser's achievements.
#RightWingConspiracy 'Normal' behavior – The abuser does everything to regain control and keep the victim in the relationship. They may act as if nothing has happened, or turn on the charm. This peaceful phase may give the victim hope that the abuser has really changed this time.
#JusticeDemocrats #PeoplesSummit #Indivisible In the cycle of abuse, the abuser's apologies and

supportive gestures in between the episodes of abuse can make it difficult to leave. They may make you believe that only you can help them, that things will be different this time, and that you are truly valued. However, the dangers of staying are very real. So get therapy. Then. leave.

Note: I lifted and massaged diagnostic language from half dozen websites about domestic, physical and emotional abuse.

— DeNeice Kenehan

The air you breathe, the water you drink, the road you drive on, the wages you make, the taxes you pay, the oceans you enjoy, the trees you love, the wars you fight, the pets you have, the education you receive- EVERYTHING IS POLITICS. Go vote today.

— Tania Singh

The **American** dream, backed by Capitalism, is just a lie to get a majority of the people worked to death while a select few reap the rewards.

— Tahbarri Clendinen

The Ecuadorian government's depriving Julian Assange of his online connections with the outside world starts the final purge of dissenters. By ignoring this violation of Assange's right to free speech, and by continuing to demonize him as a Russian agent, mainstream liberals have shown which side they stand on this purge. We have no allies within the political establishment-the death machine is ready to put the fist down onto us, and there's no telling who Assange will be followed by.

— Rainer Shea, from his article

The elephant in the room is that the United States is the most militarily aggressive, self-serving nation on Earth. We maintain hundreds of military bases worldwide. Why? China doesn't. Russia doesn't. We spend obscene amounts of money on our armed forces to the detriment of health care, education, and infrastructure. We claim we're protecting our interests abroad, but who protects the rest of the world from us? We frequently engage in war for profit at the behest of the military industrial complex and the fossil fuel conglomerates. The United States is no longer a representative democracy. It is a corporation with an army, and now an imbecilic would-be fascist dictator holds court in the White House, with the fate of civilization hanging in the balance.

— Harold Meyer

Capitalism Must Be Composted

The elite live in constant fear that the great body of people below them will one day become conscious of the systematic injustice being inflicted upon them and their children.

— James Kinsella

T **he finer things** in life are great, but 'best' rules. If something needs to be done very well, the best way to do that is to read as much as you can about it. Fortunately, experts already exist as you read this, and we can ask them how to, for example, 'lead the political world best,' or 'how to be the best diplomat because ruling with violence and fear isn't nearly as sustainable as ruling with love, compassion, and respect.' In America, the people are supposed to make the political decisions. In order to have an effective democracy, we need as many good people as we can to read about our world. Don't rely on everyone else doing it. YOU are responsible. How many millions more will suffer because you and many others sit there in apathy?

Vote every time, educate yourself about politics that you can affect, join a campaign for a good person and hold them accountable, get elected, be a good fucking person. Don't do everything. Just do something. Everyone makes waves; your shitty day can influence others' moods and consequently their decisions. Giving up and committing suicide must be the last resort; we can fight the corrupt as long as we have working hearts, brains, and guts. Never feel alone in the fight for our rights: political revolutionaries are gearing up all across America. We CAN have affordable, proper medicine for all. We CAN eliminate the super wealthy through implementation of a maximum wage. We CAN be empathetically conscious of our fellow citizens to the point of AT LEAST housing, food, and clean water for all. Although many people suck, fight for yourself at least. Fight for your mother. Fight for the oppressed orphan who must choose between rent and food. Forgive ignorance occasionally. Let's imprison the war criminals, spread the wealth, and invigorate green energy. When we stand before God's Judgement, let's have something great to argue for our souls. Do it for the children in war torn countries that will forget what it's like to have family.

A shred of humanity is all I ask from you. Commit to an hour of volunteering for goodness, especially if you're feeling depressed on a normal day (compassion makes people feel better!) You don't have to tell anyone that you read this article; treat yourself first, by all means, but please commit yourself to some kind of thing to better your community, Palestine, or any of the less fortunate.

— Sa'ad Ibm Dawud

The **Millennials**, my generation, was left behind a long time ago. I don't fight for things like tuition free college, higher wages, single payer healthcare or housing, food and water as a right in the world's richest economy for myself nor do I think I'll ever benefit from any of those things. I fight so that Generation Z, my siblings and other young people, could have the chance my generation struggled to get. Is no one else broken on the inside while hearing about our elders rationing pills? Is no one ashamed at how we treat immigrants in a country founded by immigrants? Is no one else broken over the chaos in our society leading to the school shootings and the racial tensions? I am. I don't want them to go through what we did. I want a future that doesn't mirror the present. I'll be 30 in 5 years. I don't want to reach half a century 20 years later knowing I left the next generation to the same fate mine faced without at least trying to change something. We can do better. We have to.

— Tahbarri Clendinen

Capitalism Must Be Composted

The police arrested a kid on the street searched the car with no warrant. Tell your kids to straighten up. They are needing to fill the beds in the private prison system. Remember! Everything Hitler did was legal!

— Debra Petton Bell

The poor are poor for many reasons, but the biggest reason--and it's been this way forever--is because those in power choose for them to be. They need--always at the ready--people to fight their wars, build their roads and take care of their kids and lawns.

— Debra Cusick

T**he propaganda** we have been fed for decades about single payer healthcare is baseless bullshit. We are the ONLY advanced nation that doesn't include healthcare as a RIGHT of all people, because corporations which profit off of human suffering control a majority of our politicians.

— Lani Krewson

The sad but awful truth about today's neoliberal, Wall Street, Big Business dominated Democratic Party is that it would rather lose to a pathetic con man like Donald Trump than let the progressive wing win with Bernie Sanders.

— Bert Wolfe

The Statue of Liberty should read, 'Welcome to America. We're hypocrites, our children aren't safe and the water might have lead in it. Don't ask questions.'

— Tahbarri Clendinen

The United Corporations of America is an export business. Our specialties are weapons, conflict and slavery. Take all the time you need to think about that.

— Keisha Walker

Capitalism Must Be Composted

There are a lot of folks in the U.S. who don't vote Democrat, Republican, or Libertarian. Folks who are organizing at the community level. Folks who are organizing for socialism. Folks who put people before profit. They have families, work, tremendous debt, and they are doing what they can to defeat the barbarism of capitalism. Those are the troops I support. Those are the troops I want to march with. Those are the troops I love. Revolutionaries.

— Mimi Soltysik

There is one topic in the United States that is banned from Television. We see ads every day that shows us endless consumption. We see ads from companies like the Koch brother empire and BP (British Petroleum) that sale us on the death of mankind and the end of the planet. With the Koch empire selling us on its product from destroying the lungs of the earth to toxins made from its petroleum industry. BP is saying they will not destroy the gulf, until the next time. TransCanada ripping up native territories to sell us the most toxic sludge on the planet. But they make it look good and so helpful to not give your grandchildren a future. But we keep buying it as they sell us on endless, unsustainable consumption. Energy companies are hijacking our chances to save the world by all but making solar and wind illegally to private homeowners. To banning off the grid housing and water collection by telling you don't have a right to clean water. But you can buy the water in plastic bottles that contaminate the water with cancer-causing dioxins and make their way to the oceans to kill off sea life. Saying carbon dioxide is good because it can mix with ocean water and serialize life in the oceans by making acids with the CO and CO_2.

Yet there is one topic this predatory capitalism culture does not endlessly invade your life with. Something that would cost TV hosts that pay their news infotainment personal their multimillion-dollar per year jobs. And it would disrupt this toxic soup we call western civilization. The civilization that has more guns per capita than any other country in the world. Even raining down on you Geo-engineering death from the skies by spraying toxins they can't get rid of any other way mixed with aluminum. Aluminum that stunts the growth of plants and is now being found in the brains of bees. To putting poisons in the water and telling you it is good for you. Allowing the brains neurotoxin of lead and higher rates of radioactive contamination just because another nuclear power plant melted down. The civilization that says everyone must have a gun because more people will die if there are more guns available to everyone. We can have that grand shootout with undetectable militarized drones that will blow your wedding party to smithereens. They even tell you that we need to get rid of job-killing regulations, better known as consumer protections, because why should your government keep you safe. And in this early death causing toxic way of life, can you say what that topic that is banned from television is?

Even Stephen William Hawking has warned us how unsustainable our way of life is and the so-called phantom freedoms the United States brings to us. Stephen says we are close to the tipping point of causing our own death. But all the above are those Christian values the politicians always tell you about. Believe it or not, the leading cause of death is not autoerotic asphyxiation. Mystical Christian that is, no other mythology is allowed. You are even more likely to be killed by a mass-murdering unhinged white terrorist than being struck by lightning in the United States. Even more likely than you are being killed by a foreign terrorist. But we are programmed daily by these mass-murdering death spiral advertising that we all subsidize with our tax dollars while the richest among us pay nothing in taxes. But we will gladly buy these toxins that are more dangerous than cigarettes in all our products and eat GMO toxic foods on a daily basis that cause higher rates of cancer and allergic reactions to normal foods.

Giving tax cuts to the world's worst actors, the rich, is more important than giving you the healthcare you need or an education, or even a living wage. Even more important than protecting your rights that nature gives you as a human being. Not one commercial to put down your credit card. The topic is Buy Nothing Day or Week. Oh no mister bill, we can interrupt the angle of death called the unstainable western culture. We have to frack under your home to get that last drop of gas and pollute your drinking water so you have to buy bottled water. Besides if your home blows up because of a gas leak, it is cheaper to blow you up than to regulate anything that protects consumers.

— Chuck Mullin

There is so much cognitive dissonance around this one gangly Australian not so much for the things that he has done, but for what his existence means. If our institutions were as trustworthy and just as we pretend they are, there would be no such phenomenon as Julian Assange. His reason for rising to notoriety wouldn't exist, his publications would be redundant, and his persecution wouldn't occur. If we really lived in a free and democratic society with a transparent and open government, he would have nothing to leak and no one would care if he did anyway, because our institutions would operate as advertised. These fairytales we mutter to ourselves in order to keep reality at bay must come to an end. We are not children anymore. The veils of lies and wishful thinking must be torn down and reality must be met on its terms. If you want the world to change, you have to see it for what it is otherwise you are merely impotently shrieking at your own illusory nightmares. Tear down the veils of cognitive dissonance and you will see that not only is Julian Assange living proof that things are not as advertised, but that his liberation is one of the first steps we must take towards our own liberation from the chains we woke up to find ourselves in.

— Caity Johnstone

T **here's no going** back now. One of the KXL leaked yesterday. The people in Yemen will continue to die. The environment and ecosystem will continue to collapse. The Republican and Democratic leaders of this nation will continue to extract all the wealth from the poorest and most destitute in order to enrich themselves and their donors. The democrats will pretend like they can impeach Trump even though they can't because they want you to believe that they are on the side of the people even though they aren't. They just allowed banks and payday lenders to prey on the poorest even further and to no end. Earthquakes and natural disasters will continue and people will continue to die on that front as well. I'm sure the republicans and democrats will approve the keystone XL pipeline as well. They'll tell you it's safe just like they did with all the other ones even though they weren't. They will continue to drill in the arctic and destroy the environment. There's absolutely no way we're going to come back from this. I'm done. I don't even know how you can look at your kids. I can't. Teaching people how to perform their civic duties accomplished absolutely nothing when their leaders are hard-pressed to fuck them over. All you've done is allowed this continue. I apologize to everyone. I have a child too. It sucks. This is the way it is.

— Stevie Eevee

They keep us uneducated so we don't recognize the enemy. They keep us poor so we keep working. They keep us sick so we can't fight back. They keep us confused so we keep fighting amongst ourselves.

— Tania Singh

This country is being run (into the ground) by a herd of insane, greedy sons of bitches, who have anti-nuclear shelters already built and stocked to survive there for decades. From there, they will watch us all die in a nuclear inferno of the war that they started. And we, the sheeple, will meekly allow it.

— Margaret Stringer

Capitalism Must Be Composted

This is a battle between us and the bourgeoisie and it cannot be fought through votes. If we didn't get to vote for Universal Healthcare despite widespread appeal, if we didn't get to vote for public college, if we didn't get to vote on the DAPL, if we don't get to vote against exploitative oil wars what's there for me to believe that voting is going to make a shit's worth of bloody difference when it comes to the president? They made it clear during the primaries how they feel about not drinking their Kool-Aid. How they feel about not taking bribes from Wallstreet. Why should I believe it's going to be any different the hundredth time around?

— Paul McDonald

This is a love story. But not the kind you might be expecting. It's a love story...for Standing Rock. This memory we, as a nation, have long jettisoned. A year ago, today. Indigenous people took a peaceful, prayerful stand. And were backed by non-indigenous, who learned to shut up, and listen. The movement will go down in history, as one of the most beautiful, and poignant things in this nation. This is a love story for all of those brave and momentarily thwarted warriors, those who remained peaceful, despite being infiltrated, egged on, gassed, water-cannoned, arrested, stalked, driven off the road. This is a love story, for being humbled. Beyond anything I had previously imagined. It was hard. It was worth it. And it's hard to forgive myself for being sick, and failing our case to an extent (which isn't over, by the way), but I'm trying.

This is a love story. For this new moon. For hopes we dare not hope, and dreams, we dare not dream. It is a love story, for skies in New Mexico that behave like the sea. Always changing. A wild, wild sky, that I can only breathe in. It is a love story, for the lost, and the lonely, and the broken. For those who have nothing left. For those who face their endings. This is a love story. For friends, for lovers, past and present, for those who walked away. And most especially, for those abandoned. And for those who made catastrophic mistakes.

It's a love story, for the depths of the heart, and the depths of loss we face. It doesn't matter if it is a story of triumph, or defeat. The universe, god, the everything - they don't care about this. Our defeat is as loved as our victory.

Is this weird to say? My twenty-something self would have said 'fuck yeah!' I would have thought I was weak. Oh...if only I'd known, what was coming. This isn't defeat. In the great, grand, spinning, light-speck filled scheme of things, it's not defeat. When we are too attached to ego, that fact carries little solace. But when we live at the margins, or in the chasms, in the dark caverns of poverty, or oppression, or chronic illness, or ongoing loss, and we are intrepid - of heart and soul - that fact looms large. It fills my breathing cavity. I am full, I am oh, so full, of what is.

And so, this is a love story. It is a paean to the lost and the broken, to the hopeless and the terrified. It is a paean to trying, and failing, to not trodding upon - no matter what. It is a paean to the man in rags on the sidewalk, and a hymn to that powerful woman-being who sang out into the museum's ether 'WE ARE STILL HERE! WE ARE STILL HERE!' It is paean to those who have nothing left. And nothing left, to give.

This love story, even if I lose everything, even if I am denied the love of my heart, and my greatest hopes, it is a love story, to living. To having had this time, and sung this song, and known, known, known, even if for an ephemeral and blinding minute, to have KNOWN, love. I will go where many have quietly trod. I will fall. I will get up again, or not. I will not call upon the gods. I will call upon the truth, dormant and vibrating, in the depths of my cells. I will call on love, and this love story, for us all. May we be undeniably held, in ways that we never dared dream, nor expected.

This is a love story. To nonviolent revolutionaries, and to paradigm shifters, and to the most broken and discarded, of us all. And no matter what it looks like on the outside, it is still, it will always be, beautiful.

— Tangerine Bolen

This is what I would vote for. Income equality, CEO pay no more than 20x the lowest paid employee. Banning all corporate money in politics with no more than 10,000 per person that can be donated to a campaign. Banning all lobbying money. You can still have a progressive lobbyist that represent the people but no corporate lobbyist or foreign government lobbies. Ban gerrymandering, implement civilian distracting, ban super-delegates, ban the electoral college, Implement cross-party ranked-choice voting, all voters get mail-in ballots, banning voting machines, ban provisional ballots, civilian over-site hand counting and reporting of vote counts and data entry into the ranked-choice voting. All changes to the tax and budgets must be decided by the people through a voting process. legislators can no longer decide how taxpayer money is spent. Kickbacks from corporations public or private banned. Implement a multi-party parliament, more than just two, a party gets 3% of the vote they get 3% of the seats in parliament. Basic minimum income, healthcare for all through the Medicare system without premiums and copays. A ban on all fossil fuels, Hemp legal, all natures plants legal, and implement nature's rights to be the same as human rights.

Decriminalize all drugs, addiction is a health problem, not a criminal problem. Immediate release of all non-violent and victimless criminals ban on death penalty. All criminal are still civilians and keep all rights even the right to vote. A living wage for minimum wage. A ban on billionaires, Tax of 75% on incomes over 1 million dollars. Low-income housing. Tax on all stock market transactions, stock market banks separate from deposit banking and all insurance separate from banks. Bankers in jail. Break up big banks, State banks, and community banking. Employ own corporations and worker co-ops. No centralized banking. Tax on all goods coming into the country to offset the price it cost to make the good in the country.

Demilitarize the police and demand protection of people over private property. The public paid schools, colleges, and universities. A full ban on unregistered guns, requiring licensing with 4 year renewal, and liability insurance on all guns, ban on all guns holding more than 6 bullets, a complete ban on all civilian owned militarized weapons require biometric trigger locks. End all wars and colonialism. End of government deciding to go to war, all wars voted on by the general public. A complete ban on all arms sales, and tax money going to foreign countries. End to all corporate subsidies, except for clean non-nuclear energy and nature restoration.

Every human civilization has the right to clean air, land and Living water, see Viktor Schauberger for the meaning of living water. A representative of the people can receive no money except for the salary the people decide to give them, they cannot keep campaign money, a complete ban on any corporate or banking involvement in government punishable by organized crime laws. A complete ban on all corporate owned or involved press, News organizations must be nonprofits and unbiased. Each item in treaties must be decided on by the public, and the treaty must be voted on by the public. All treaties even Native American treaties must be honored. If any study shows the actions of the government or corporations or business could harm the next 7 generations of humans, that action should be stopped, and this should expand to 49 generations of human beings.

— Chuck Mullin

T his old woman, maybe 70ish was just in the store talking about, 'I just don't understand how working people are supposed to survive these days.' I was like, 'Yeah, it's tough.' She goes, 'Richest country in the world. It's just wrong.' I said, 'Well, the rich are doing alright.' She says, 'That's what you get when you elect rich people. Rich people helping rich people.' As she was leaving she turned and said, 'They're gonna get what's coming to them, one way or the other.' So, I'm still just standing here like, 'Holy shit. Comrade Granny.'

— Mat Mason

To all **my friends** fighting in the Revolution... Although, the Facebook memories from the past 2 years, that pop up in our feed every day, can be painful and heartbreaking...They also prove we were right about EVERY DAMN THING. We turned off our TV's, refused to be told how to think by the rich and powerful, and we did our research. We bucked the system, then, and continue to fight the system, now. KEEP FIGHTING, you're still right, EVERY DAMN DAY.

— Anita Daniel

To those who never knocked on a door, never phone banked, never donated money they couldn't afford, never marched in a protest, never spent their vacation days sitting on the capitol steps, never showed outrage over Standing Rock, never sent money for supplies for water protectors, never organized grassroots fundraisers, never did a GAWD DAMN THING...but, show up at the polls every four years to vote for a lesser evil, and tell everyone else how it wasn't polite to talk about politics. THANK YOU, for the many condescending lectures I've received over the past year, about what it means to be a great American, and how I need to think to be a 'good' person.

— Anita Daniel

Ugh. I watched the body cam footage from the now fired Baton Rouge police officer who shot and killed Alton Sterling. I was struck by the utter disrespect this officer showed Mr. Sterling from the moment of first encounter. I HIGHLY doubt that a white man in the same circumstances would've been talked to and treated with such disrespect. It was disgusting. And that was BEFORE Mr. Sterling was tased and then shot to death while asking what the heck was going on. And then, the body cam shows a bunch of white officers dealing with the aftermath while this officer curses Mr. Sterling as he lays dead or dying.

— Verna Averell

Under this system of unfettered capitalism, inequality, and exploitation, human beings have become disposable commodities. We have entered a post-human nightmare. Everything you do to affirm the HUMANITY of yourself and others in this dark era is an act of rebellion against the coming Extinction.

— Joan Hunter Iovino

Capitalism Must Be Composted

U suary, thievery, larceny, austerity, trickery, snobbery, dishonesty, fakery, gluttony, elitism, sadism, hedonism, cronyism, neo-liberalism, corporatism, treason, murder, greed, fraud, deceit, corruption, vileness, meanness, hatefulness ....

— RA Robertson, on why Democratic donations are drying up

We allowed Nazi soldiers that we had held in POW camps... to immigrate here legally after the war.... and there are little old grandmas being carted off to places they can't even remember... little kids shipped into immigration detention centers for god knows how long... and then off to war-torn countries that WE ruined... just for a little perspective, guys.

— Julie Hickey

Capitalism Must Be Composted

We play a dangerous game when we accuse activists involved in movements to change this world of ours of being pawns of one political party or the other. We know how the Dems pick up on every issue that is pissing people off and how they use it for their own benefit. We know how the Republicans use religion and their false morals to sway people to vote against individual rights. But to accuse students protesting violence in schools of being pawns of the DNC is so harmful and degrading. To say that young people are ignorant and don't know what they are doing when they take to the streets is a horrible policy. Do you think that of those who protested the Vietnam War or promoted the Civil Rights Movement of the 60's? Were they too young and stupid to accomplish anything as you say the young people of today are? Are those who criticize the students rallying against guns in school also going to criticize those who rally against the fossil fuel industry? Are all activists puppets to you? Be careful what you say especially when you accuse activists of being puppets for the DNC because that is not how it works at all. If we are going to label activists as being pawns for a political party then we may as well give in and give up and sit at home and wait for the end to come.

— Angela Basta

We the people are just the lab rats watching the experiments and waiting for the next needle, wheel, surgery and hoping for death as the Nazis and the corporations walk in and out among our tiny cages, wringing their hands and smirking with glee.

— Ellen O'Donohue

Capitalism Must Be Composted

Wealthy capitalists have built a winning system for themselves. They love the work week when all the workers provide cheap labor for corporations to exploit, and they also love weekends when workers have time to go out and spend what little money they earned on overpriced products, creating even more profit for the capitalists.

— Estela Jordan

What are we celebrating? The fact that innocent lives are being taken by the very people that are supposed to protect us, the fact that our education system sucks, the fact that our country is bombing innocent lives and causing instability in countries across the world, the fact that we have the most incarcerated people in the world, or the fact that our country was built on indigenous lands because of genocide and on black slavery? Don't get me wrong America does have many great opportunities and I am privileged to be here. I am proud to be born in a country where I can take advantage of the resources they have to better the lives of my family and those around me, but this country has a lot of fxcking work to do. You can't seriously be proud of where this country is right now. And for those of you who are thinking 'if you don't like it here then leave,' you can't blame me for wanting what's best for everyone both in our country and abroad.

— Bella Chavez

Capitalism Must Be Composted

W**hen I was** quite fucking rudely awakened last year by the BLATANT AND OBVIOUS corruption of the Democratic Party, I promised I would never forget, and I won't. I will never lose my sense of outrage. Ever. I WILL keep hope in brighter days. I will work to heal from the ptsd that the fraudulent 2016 US election left behind. All the Dems do is prove to me daily that I made the right choice. I won't ever look back. I feel very free of the chains that once bound me. I believe that we can and will create a new party that will bring us together and help us heal as a country. Birthing pains. Eyes on the prize people. Hearts ablaze. Fight on.

— Ella Dani

When people say that #Seattle is a 'socialist hellhole,' what they really mean is that it's a place where the inherent contradictions of capitalism have become so untenable they can't be fixed with the same tools that precision-engineered the crisis. It's like if your house burnt down and your main complaint is that the firefighters caused too much water damage.

— Brett Hamil

When **Trayvon** Martin and Michael Brown were murdered and people were threatening to burn Ferguson, MO down, people were told to protest peacefully because 'the message was being lost in the chaos.' People also said not to jump to conclusions because there was no video proof of what happened to Trayvon. Philando Castile gets murdered on camera and people once again react. This time the reason against the protests were because highways were being blocked. Finally, we reach the football players and some Americans, 'taking a knee,' in protests against police brutality. Mind you, many more have died since Philando Castile. However, no broken windows. No highways blocked. No fires...and people are still mad at the protesters? Trayvon Martin was murdered 5 years ago and every time someone has died from police brutality since then, we've been told to change the way we protest. If you're going to complain, gripe and moan about the most PEACEFUL way people have protested yet, GET OUT OF THE WAY OF PROGRESS. We've got a country to change and your negativity is NOT wanted. It didn't start with Trayvon and if we don't address police brutality, someone else will become a hashtag. STOP pretending you love America by defending the militarized police force.

— Tahbarri Clendinen

When you're young you tell yourself comforting little lies about how it'll be better one day. But then u grow up and realize that's just a delusion and bc u exist in a system of economic slavery and vulture capitalism and the only escape is death. Ijs have a nice day. Happy fucking Monday.

— Jessie Memer

Capitalism Must Be Composted

W **hether from** Bernie's movement, Occupy, or their own experiences, there's a growing segment of the American left who will never cast their vote for a corporate-owned candidate again. Thank you ALL for staying strong and fighting back!!! The people's revolution. The parties need to wake the fuck up.

— Perry Wheeler

Y **esterday I** realized how deeply I hate the US empire for destroying the Middle East, now North Africa, and pushing against the border of Russia and havoc in the Asian Sea. I think all our other problems including healthcare, education, immigration etc. are intertwined with this. And intertwined for sure is our humanity, our core value system, our empathy or lack of it for others and how our taxes and our government's actions impact the lives of others all over the planet.

— Suzanne Thurston

Capitalism Must Be Composted

You know what's remarkable? If we lived in a country with universal healthcare, free education, a jobs program, a living wage, and a police force that existed to actually protect and serve, it might make sense why most people are comfortably numb and not fighting their oppression. But, considering that we have none of those things, we indiscriminately bomb sovereign nations purely for greed, our government is run by criminals and lunatics (red and blue alike), and we're losing our constitutional rights left and right, it's mind-boggling that we're not taking it to the streets on a daily basis until we affect real change.

— Elif Love

List of Contributors

Allen, Ruth 20
Alpert, Dave 34
Anthony, Michael 21, 24
Austin Dunham, Amy 60
Avarell, Verna 148
Barker, William 13
Basta, Angela 65, 152
Black Elk, Linda 39
Blanchard, Patricia 111
Boheler, Andrew 55
Bolen, Tangerine 80, 139
Bosma, Laurel 99
Brown, Stephanie 58
Burris, Beverly 91
Bush, Michelle 45
Canada, Mike 42
Carbon, Barb Moose ix
Cecilia, Sarah 6
Chapman, Kate 41
Chavez, Bella 155
Clendinen, T. **92, 106, 117, 123, 128, 158**
Collins, Elizabeth 52
Conklin, Patrick 43
Connor, Emily 107
Cusick, Debra 125
Dani, Ella 156
Daniel, Anita 146, 147
Davis, Jake 11
Dawud, Sa'ad Ibm 121
Dye, Jason 5
Eevee, Stevie 85, 135
Einer, Lee 88
Elderton, Mary Beth 36
Frene, Teresa 9, 54
Gilder, Jennifer 68
Gonzalez, Joseph 62
Grose, Alan 110
Hamil, Brett 157
Hatfield, Barbara 78
Havener, Timothy 2, 15, 28
Hellén, Kristoffer 66
Herzoff, Evan 95
Hickey, Julie 10, 151
Iovino, Joan Hunter 149
Isabel, Fiorella 109
Jaroch, Joseph 12
Johnstone, Caity 134
Jordan, Estela 154
Kahn, Whitney 83
Kendall, Bonnie 104
Kenehan, DeNeice 113
King, Bryant 69

Kinsella, James 120
Krewson, Lani 126
Lambe, Laurie 74
Landon, Tanette 32
Leutwyler, Matthew 17, 93
Love, Elif 162
Lynch, Warren 96
Lyons, Chelsea 89
MacGregor, Reidun 108
Mannarino, Carol 35
Mason, Mat 145
Matthews, Adrian 87
Mcbard, Maryann 37
McDonald, Paul 138
Memer, Jesse 159
Meyer, Harold 119
Michael, Sam 84
Mitchell, Matt 7
Mucci, Jay 101
Mullin, Chuck 131, 142
Nimmo, Susan 100
O'Donohue, Ellen 153
Pantenburg, Sharon 76
Petton Bell, Debra 50, 124
Phillips, Lorraine 38
Photiades, Stefanos 97
Pierre, Frantz 70

Predmore, Joe 22
Reeves, J.d. 23
Rigby, Jim 33, 77
Robertson, RA 150
Rockstroh, Phil 18
Ruzgis, Patricia 103
Sankara, Lola 71
Schultz, Elizabeth 75
Scott, Guy 25
Sexauer, Linda Carpenter 46, 112
Shea, Rainer 72, 118
Sheared, Tanya 26
Shibabaw, Teddy 49
Singh, Tania 3, 53, 56, 90, 116, 136
Skolnick, Ryan 8
Soltysik, Mimi 67, 86, 130
Stringer, Margaret 137
Sullivan, Fred 16
Thurston, Suzanne 161
Tiernan, Cullen 73
Walker, Keisha 129
Walton, Lisa 98
Wheeler, Perry 160
Wolfe, Bert 127
Wright, Mike 51
Yo, Maurice 82

About the editor

Ruth is an activist in Seattle where she lives and tries to join forces with other progressives when possible. She has been known to spend a lot of time on social media and like any typical Seattleite likes coffee, beer, and oatmeal – not in that order. Find Ruth at her weblog: *ruthoskolkoff.wordpress.com*

About the artist

Sneha is an activist in New York City. Her daytime expertise is managing non-profit marketing projects and at night and on weekends, she explores her artistic skills as a form of therapy. You can find Sneha passionately sharing her views, thoughts, and compiled educational materials on Instagram at: *instagram.com/snaybelle*

Made in the USA
Coppell, TX
12 August 2021